TIFFANY GIBBS

Words to My God

GIBBS PUBLISHING
CONGLOMERATE

First published by Gibbs Publishing Conglomerate 2014

Second edition

ISBN: 978-1-966856-03-0

This book was professionally typeset on Reedsy.
Find out more at reedsy.com

Contents

Acknowledgments

I dedicate this book to my first love – His name is Jesus. You were with me as a little girl and though I went into the world for a time, I never forgot your name. Thank you for never forgetting mine and for calling me back into the fold.

Thank you to my home church, Crown of Glory Ministries and especially my pastors, Apostle Donald and Prophetess Judith Peart. Pastor Judy - thank you for your prayers, your love, your hugs, and your mother's heart. Thank you for encouraging me in the gifts God has given me. Pastor Donald – thank you for your revelation knowledge, wisdom, and for providing a safe haven. You have taught me (and countless others) so much about the Word and about how to conduct oneself as a disciple of Christ. Your lives are a blessing!

Thank you to my family. I love you all. Thank you for encouraging my love of reading and writing at a very early age.

There are many more that have encouraged me during the years. Even if I have not mentioned you by name, please know that I appreciate you all!

Introduction

This book is for any person that found themselves looking for love, acceptance, and understanding in the people, places, and things of this world. We have not even begun to grasp the depth, the width, the length and the height of God's love for us. [Ephesians 3:18] These are my words to my God. I hope you will see my journey in my words – and maybe see some similarities to your own. I am not perfect but birthed through the love of a perfect Man.

Where Only God Remains

I want to go to a place
A place where only God remains
A place where I am named His
And I am whole
And I am healed

I want to go to a place
Where only God remains
Because I am the reason His Son was slain
Because of Him, I no longer hold any blame

I want to be free
To be all He made me to be
Not a slave to circumstance
Not bound by wrong romance
I want Him to be my King
I want it to be
just He and Me

Because I know
That the Father, Son, and Spirit
Are enough

I wish the world could believe

Sometimes I grieve
And I fight against the healing taking place in me
I groan
And the tears fall
And He puts me back together again

In those moments of vulnerability
It is just He and Me
And I reach that place where everything is out
In a pile of defilement
Laid at His feet
And this is the place
When I am emptied and pleading to be filled
That only God remains

I Choose You

I choose You
In the midst of the storm
I call on You

My prayer is that I am recognized
Among those who cry out
Because I choose You

Because You are all I ever wanted
And You were all I ever needed
Before I even realized what it meant
I choose You

And in all the rejection
And the things I subjected myself to
You reached out Your hand
And You chose me too

Before breath was breathed into my lungs
You set in me a purpose
That now I am struggling to remember
And in the confusion I know one thing

I choose You

And the world is jealous for me
It pulls, weighs me down as I reach up
But Your touch
It thrusts me forward
And I choose You

When they say I love You too much
I ask them do they know You?
Because if they did
They'd love You too

And I'll carry my cross of persecution
And they can mock me if they like
Because I choose You.

Alien

One day, I won't feel like an alien in this skin
I'll inhale and know it's me
And there's no other way God or I should have it be

I'll love every dimple in all of my cheeks
And I'll smile at the crease in my forehead
Those days that I thought I'd be better off …
Well those days will be overshadowed by grace

And I'll love every imperfection in my face
Every scar, scratch, wrinkle will be something
That makes my eyes twinkle
I'll love it because it's mine
And I love it because God put it there
And He thinks I'm fine

I'm a masterpiece
And if I stand out
It's because I'm set apart

So if I'm foreign, alien even
I guess that's just the space I'm in

The cross I carry
The mercy in which I sit
I can't help if I'm different

Reaching Out

Reaching out, just to hold
Wanting warmth but coming up cold
Trapped within
Seek release
Hurt and frustrated
With no relief

At night the loneliness
Stealing sleep
Reaching out
Longing for something to keep

A stranger in skin
No recognition
And denied by all
Struggling to breathe
Reaching out
For someone to call

And yet
No one sees
My hands are reaching

Yet others seem blind to me
Kneeling down
Say a prayer
My comfort comes from above
My Father was always there

Anoint Me

Anoint me
Touch me with your soul
Remind me of what I missed
Help me to remember
What it is to be whole

Anoint me
With your presence
And bless me with your kiss
Remind me of the loving
That I so badly missed

Anoint me
With your love
And your heart, spirit, and mind
Hold me close
Tell me you'll always be mine

Anoint me
With a union that is holy
A kiss that will never die
A promise of a lifetime

Tell me you'll always be mine

Anoint me
With your presence
Anoint me
With your soul
Give me something stable
Something I can hold

In a world filled with uncertainty
In love I wish for the divine
A union anointed by the Most High
A union that surpasses life
A union that triumphs over death
A love that will live beyond my last breath

Hey Love

Hey Love,
I am in a place of incubation
Being healed and made new
Revitalized and I realize
All the mistakes I made in dealing with you

Hey Love,
I apologize for not being whole
Before seeking you
And due to the holes in my logic
I let you slip through

Hey Love,
I have grown past the drama
I have let go of the trauma
That plagued my heart and mind
I am discovering a greater Love
Than any man can provide

Hey Love,
My heart is stronger
And the voids are being filled

When I meet you again
I'll recognize who you really are
Impostors will be stopped at the door

Now that I know the Father
I know you
Now I know how to tell if you are true
Love, I am waiting
I know when we meet
This time it will be good
Hey Love,
I'm here
I'm almost ready for you.

Broken, Beautiful

For so long
Felt like I was broken
Never fit
Always fearful
Ever lonely
Wanting more of something

And then in my brokenness
I was beautiful
And new
And humbled
And lifted up

And His hands are putting the pieces
Back together
And making the crocked places straight
My countenance reflects His glory
And my faith
It makes me whole

I can take off the mask
I can show you who I am

Because I believe first that I am His

Once a broken, earthly vessel
I am made into something more
Much more significant
The first intention

In my brokenness
I find out who I am
Who I am to be
And who I always was

I am not who you think
I am more
I am not what you see
I am more
I am loved
I am treasured
I am no longer broken
But each day renewed and made whole

I am beautiful
And I am bold
And I peel back the layers
To see what else lies just below

Finally
I am beginning to love
My reflection

Wilderness

You take me through the wilderness
Through cold and loneliness
I'm tempted with the wonders of the world
But I know nothing compares to You

And sometimes I feel forsaken
Why have you left me here?
I know that I am just passing through
But I feel so naked, so bare

All the things I fear
And all the things I feel
Recognizing that these things are not real

And I know as I meander through
You watch over
And I am guarded on all sides
Because though I'm in the wilderness
Your light is still my guide

I am not forsaken
And I will not always feel so alone

You want me to come closer
To realize You are my home

This is just a part of my journey
This walk through a barren land
I see you waiting at the other end
With outstretched hands…

Island

I am that mountain peak
That emerges from the ocean
I grow and shift and evolve
And He is the water that surrounds it all

Separating me unto Himself
Comforting me in my loneliness
Sometimes longing to be a part of the larger mass
But knowing it is my destiny to be different
Set apart
Just for Him

And daily He washes me
And reminds me of His love
His love laps over my banks
And the breeze from His waters
Soothes me

It was a miracle I was even formed
Explosions and eruptions built me
And when I emerged
My soil was fertile

Fit to support life
When the lava cooled
I was something new

His waves carved my shape
Defined my shores
And though I am an island
I feel secure
Daily He washes me
And reminds me of His love

The Hope

I carry on with the hope
That I will be so much more than my circumstance
And the promises spoken over me
Before I was in my mother's womb are true

The hope of a life not marred by rejection
Addiction to the man that makes my knees weak
And his love, it beats me senseless
And I won't always be so reckless

The hope that I am not alone in the world
And that the still, small voice that whispers
Encouragement to me is not my own
That a man could love me so much He died for me
The man would not try to hurt me

The pain of not enough…
Love Hugs Acceptance
Numbed by lust drugs and pestilence
The hope that I can be washed clean
Of these defiling things

God said "Seek Me and ye shall find me"
And "I will give your soul rest"
Oh how I run toward Jesus
With the hope of grace and life eternal

Into arms that comfort
And do not molest
Into arms that offer a sweet caress
And my heart cries out
Jesus! Oh how I love Him!

You are the Hope
Of a wretch like me
A Savior of my lost spirit
For the words spoken to me
Before I was in my mother's womb
Are still "Yes" and "Amen"
In you, my God
I can begin again.

Redemption

There are things I have done
And things I have seen
That I am ashamed to repeat
And yet, even from these things
I have been redeemed

From psychics to tarot cards
To sleeping with Babylon
Yet a Man loved me so much
That He atoned for these things
Before they were even done

I am so thankful for the Son
And so thankful He called me near
I remember being in the middle of the club
Hearing God speak to me
Realizing this was not the plan He had in mind

I knew it was time
Fear tried to keep me bound
I was afraid of not keeping my word to God
I was afraid of giving up the pleasures of the world

But at the end of the day I knew
I was just a broken little girl

I needed the Father, Son, and Spirit
And they beckoned to me
When I confessed His name
I knew then, I was free

As I shake off the shackles of my past life
Not perfect but striving forth
I feel a peace in my soul
I know redemption in the renewing of my mind
My past is not present when you look into my eyes
And I hope as I spend more time in God's presence
There will not even be a remnant
And when you look at me, you see Him

My Spirit Cries Out (Alabaster Box)

There were days of loneliness so profound
Each day held clouds that blotted out the Son
I was hurt and battered and tired and angry
And my spirit cried out for something more

Brokenhearted and betrayed
I wondered if the Father was really there
My spirit cried out in despair

When I said enough
There has to be more for me
I entered Your house
I heard Your truth
And I gave into Your Will

I knelt in prayer
And my spirit cried out
The tears fell harder
As He spoke to me
He said, that lonely time on the cross
His pain…He did that all for me
And I poured out all I had in praise

My tears covered his feet
Gathered where the nails had been
And I wiped the tears with my hair

I said Lord, I do not deserve you
And He whispered
I did this because I loved you even then
And my cup was full
My spirit cried out
Hallelujah!

He said my tears were like spikenard
So sweet was my praise
How could I not worship Him?
Through His sacrifice, I am made whole
And my spirit cries out
Joy!

He understood my pain
And He accepted my praise
And though I was never worthy
He saw me fit to be saved

No one will ever know except Him
I finally understand the cost
I lay my praise and worship at his feet
I am like Mary
Ever thankful
Pouring out my tears of joy
Over my Lord's feet
The oil from my little alabaster box

Disconnected

What happened to my joy?
So disconnected
My hurt and unforgiveness
Has erected a tent

Trying to tear it down
And wanting to leave the shelter
And all I can muster is sadness
Can you hear my cry?

I know You are here
But I need to feel You
I choke back the tears
Because I'm so tired of feeling

I don't want death
I just want to live through it
I want to give You the glory
When I get over

And my heart is longing for You
Because I have nothing else

I am lonely
And distressed
My God,
I feel so disconnected

Please hear my cry
I know You feel my heartache
I know this is not more than You
Would ask me to take

I forsake the world for You
But I feel like I am doing so much wrong
I am so downtrodden
That prayer is hard

I call out
Jesus, I plead Your blood over me
My God,
Please help me to reconnect

The Gift

I heard the news
And I began to weep
A precious gift
She was supposed to keep

She gave it away
Did not understand the worth
She let it go
And did not understand the price

She was paid for in blood, water, and Spirit
And her body, it was meant to be
A temple for the Most High
And she let an intruder enter
All I could do is cry

I spent my days
Working my way back to where she was
Praying for renewal of my mind
And restoration of my body

I am getting to know my Father

And I understand my own worth
But in my past
The opposite was true

I never wanted her to feel the emptiness
After the visitor leaves
The shattered gates
And painful silence

A gift
Given once
By grace restored
I weep and pray
That she will understand
And ask God to heal
And restore…

Fix Me

Lord, I could focus on how
I can be easily offended
And how deep down I want to
Be somebody special
And how I wish I saw myself
How the world sees me
Or more importantly
How You see me

And I could beat myself up
On how I argued with my friends
And how I can be impossible to convince
And how I can be sharp in temper
And worse with my tongue

Lord, I could tell you how scared
I have always been of showing how
I really feel because it was easier
To dismiss it
And easier to push it away
And easier to say I am okay
…when I'm not

And I could tell you how I tolerate
Other people going through
But I feel exposed when they see me
And I could tell you how deep down
I feel like I should be better
Because I know better…right?
But deep down, it's an issue of pride

And Lord, I could give excuses
And I could tell you why
But you already know why I cry
You already know why I hurt
So Lord, all I can ask of you is to
Fix me
Heal me

Help me to accept your love
Help me to recognize that everyone won't leave
If they see the real me
Help me to see that the real me isn't so bad
Help me to love me
Please Lord, fix me
Help me to see me like you see me
Help me to see where you want me to be
Help me to feel complete
Please Lord, fix me

Make me to be better than how I am
Help me to hear the positive
And push the negative away
Help me see that You are here to stay

Help me to not feel so insecure…

You peeled back the top layer
And exposed all my nerves
Lord, help me to trust that in this
You are healing the greater hurt
And through the vulnerability
That seems intolerable
You more than tolerate me
You love me
When I feel unlovable
You comfort me when it all seems too much
You keep my feet planted
When all I want to do is hide from myself
…and from You

I cry out,
Lord, heal me
Fix me
Help me to realize
I am already whole

Release

I screamed my anguish
And I asked God why
And I finally broke down
And let myself cry
Let myself feel all the pain
Right down to my toes
Let the pain travel up and out
From deep in my soul
And I let it out in one great release
Surprised that there is any part of me left
Left to write this poem
Left to wake up each morning
Alone
But after I let the tears run and run
I wiped them away
And I knew I was finally done
I let you go
I let you cry
Let myself feel the weight of my heart's lie
Let God whisper "It'll be all right"
I released it all and my healing took root
Let love transition

Let love leave
Let love grow elsewhere
Let you go away from me.

Beautiful

There is beauty in this world
In every tear that is shed
In every smile that crosses one's lips
In every death
In every birth

We all share the same destiny
The end of our time on this earth
But there is beauty in this world
And one must live and breathe it
For all that beauty is worth

I see beauty in the sunrise
And I see God in the sunset
And I see the Spirit in children's laughter
And I see the Son in their breath

There is beauty in this world
So do not look upon it with regret
There is beauty in the struggle
It is God's way of making sure we don't forget

There is beauty in His wisdom
And the life that seemed to be taken too soon
There is beauty in His countenance
For the life that grows in a woman's womb

There is beauty in this world
And you are blind if you can't see
All the things you wish that weren't
Were always meant to be

There is beauty in this world
And for every tear I cry
I know there's a thousand more smiles
Waiting for me
By and by

Cipher

Lord, Your words play a melody
That my heart longs to hear
Lord, Your face it glows, shines over me
It removes all fear

It is more than a melody, it is more than a sound
It is the sound of Your arms around me, it is a hug, it is Your
crown
It is the feel of Your love all over me
It is an acceptance felt deep inside
It is a love that is perfect
That shines light through every cloud

You sing over me a song
That lets me know I can remove my shroud
It is a melody so quiet, yet within it is so loud
Lord, I hear Your song calling me
To stand up, accept, and be proud

And I feel my flesh run away from Thee
Your glory hangs over like a cloud
Your words bring tears to me

It is more than a sound
It is the story of my livelihood
The reason I was found
My Father is more than a song to me
Holy Spirit, help me decipher the sound

A Greater Gift

I came to you
With a sense of urgency
I knew now was the time
And this was it
I was finally ready to give myself
Ready to commit

Broken
Hurt
Confused
Empty
Wanting to be filled

Clubbing couldn't fill it
Friends couldn't fill it
Sex couldn't fix it
Because in the end
I still felt alone

And you gave me joy
The weight of you filled this vessel to overflow
And the tears fell and I let you in

That's where the trouble began

Rejection and financial distress
Feeling the defilement burned from my flesh
Even in the pain of healing and the light of knowledge
I realize you gave me
The greater gift

Consistency

I want to be consistent
But part of me is resistant
To the restraint
Of managing my time
And all the while I'm missing
The things that I am insistent
That I need to be stable in my life

I just wish I was more consistent
And I try to listen
To people who I know and trust
And God wants to thrust me
Into the position
In which He can form me
But it must be pretty annoying
That I have trouble with consistency

I try to be dependable
And diligent and flexible
But in general
I'm dependably late
And I want to be the person

To do the things I expect of others
But I feel like I just can't
Seem to get it together

I am faithful to a fault
And loyal, though imperfect
And I have knowledge in part
But, I have to take the fault
For why I am not more consistent

See, there is a wall
Somewhere in me that makes some things hard
But when I finally make it into His presence
I fall apart
My heart leaps in my chest
And I am so happy
That I pressed in
But I know I need to consistently
Be His.

Distractions and unfruitful interactions
Seem to keep me from interacting
With my Lord the way
He and I really want
I know I have to make a decision
To set down somewhere
Long enough so He can give me His vision
Maybe if I'd stop struggling to be
More consistent
And just breathe
He would finally, really

Speak to me
And tell me what I need
To heal me
To set me free
And help me to consistently trust
That God has got me
He keeps telling me
He is not like the others
And that He wants to love me like no other
If I would just consistently
Let Him in

I open up a little
And fear gets in the middle
And rejection joins in on the play
Then I wonder
Am I even worthy of His love anyway?

No one else could seem
To give me it without condition
There was always something missing
And I have learned to live with less

But if something doesn't change
I'll be consistently strained
Always in pain
And I will not get to where I want to be,
Consistently in His presence!

This is a frustrating lesson
This play on words

And the more I think on it
It seems so absurd
That the only boundary to consistency…
Is me.

My Identity

I'm trying to figure out who I am
Trying to accept who I may be
Trying to make sense of me

Who am I to You?
Do You think I'm beautiful
Do You think I'm smart enough
Do You think I am enough?

Because often times I don't
And I try to make my identity in You
The only one that matters
But I am still trying to accept what is in front of me

My expectations are earthly in nature
So of course they always fall short
I could never imagine how You see me
Then a Voice inside reminds me…

I am a manifestation of You
Everything I read about me must be true
You said that I was made but a little lower than the angels

And I was created to please You

You did not give me the spirit of fear
You did not teach me to doubt
And You are the one that can help me accept
That I am beautiful
And I am smart enough
And I am enough
Because in Your image
I was made.

Ride

I let you take my heart for a ride
Up and down and all around
And it didn't stop until you said so,
I was left waiting in line

Now, I'm letting another be my guide
HE will never hurt me
And HE will never leave me broken
HE heals and HE forgives
Through HIM I am made free

And I know now the adrenaline from your ride
Was a temporary high
Because I was still left hungering for more

But through HIM, I am made whole
And through HIM, I am made better
And through HIM, I will find my forever

I thought I had found that with you
I thought you were my prayers come to fruition
But you were just a part of my journey to HIM

I am on a ride of a different kind
Where I let GOD be my guide
And through HIM I can forgive you
And through HIM I can move on

Thirsty

So much change and so many decisions and I remember, it is
written:
"I am Alpha and Omega", the "Beginning and the end"
You have put an end to so much sin in my life
Yet I thirst

More of you in me
More of you displayed
Radiating out like the Son
and I just want to be the one
That you want to rest upon

I thirst for more of you O God
And I am tired of mediocre
In You, I would like to be great
Glorifying you and being an example of the good things
You have done

I thirst.

More of your rain
Trim the dead branches

I'll forget the pain
If you would just reign...
In my heart, forever.

I thirst like the deer, oh, my soul thirsts
For more clarity
May your waters wash away
The confusion
The endless chatter
And distraction of every. day. life.

Lord, I need You
More today than I did the day I got saved
Lord, I thirst for more
Call me by my new name

Lovely
Beautiful
Holy
Clean

I thirst for You to manifest in me
Every gift given
May it flourish, good seed in fertile soil
Lord, water me.

May I be a tree planted in you
Roots deep
Not like feet planted in sand
Deep down
In the Heavens

My roots ascend

Lord, I thirst for You
Clear all the distractions
My attraction is to You

Wash away the remnants of defilement
The denial of every lie
Let it be replaced with Truth
I now belong to You

Let my pursuit after You
Be relentless
As Your Love for me
Free
Grace
Mercy
Given
me.

Holy Spirit
Thirsting for more
Of You, in me.

Deciding To Love

I am learning that love is a decision
It takes determination
It takes vision
Love means looking past the immediate
And seeing the completion
The maturity of a man
Love is much more perfect
The more we become like He who works perfection in us
He does that the more
We resist the lust -
Eyes, flesh, pride of life
I decide to love through the stressors of life
I am determined to love through the pain
Even as you reject me
I'll decide to love again
And again I love as you hate the more
Heaping my love upon you like hot coals
And in loving, I find my joy
Not in happenstance
Not in meaningless ploys
Because my source is one greater than me
The author of love

My God, Father, Savior, Spirit
  Who delivered me

And The Time Came

And the time came
For me to emerge out of hiding
No more games
No more ducking in shame

Time to show my face again
Show God is in the place
Within me, shining
Brightly, in spite of me

And the time came
For no more fear
He promised that He would wipe
Every tear from my eye

The fighting has ceased
Because the Son lives in me
Now, the time has come
For me to receive

Every thing God has for me
Accept Christ's resurrection life as fact

Accept the finished work of the cross
Time for me to stop crawling
Time for me to walk.

For All I've Lost

Sometimes I cry
Shed a tear for a relationship lost
For a family member that can't understand
That I left them for a man
Jesus is His name
For His sake, daily
I am slain
And for all I've lost
It is my soul I've gained

I know what has been said
From the phone calls, tentative hellos
Some say I've lost all my sense
But for all I've lost
It is my sanity, my peace
I have gained

No, I am not the same
When I look in the mirror
I no longer cry
I like the smile
The eyes that reflect that I am

"fearfully and wonderfully made"
I realize this was all preordained
For all that I've lost
It is my salvation
I have gained

You may not understand
Why I don't crank that new Souljah Boy
And why I don't know that new Lil' Wayne
If they not talking about Jesus
And extending His fame
I don't know their names
See, for the latest craze I've missed
I'm all the more glad I'm saved

For all the sacrifices
And nails to my hands
The mud that covers my name
I know I die daily in my Savior's name
And for all those I've lost
I love you
But I'm happy about what I've gained.

About the Author

Tiffany Gibbs, who also writes under the name Tiffany Michele, is an author who crosses genres. Whether it be nonfiction, science fiction, or poetry, Tiffany enjoys it all. She enjoys writing books for children, as well as for young adults, and adult readers. Her love of reading started early and grew as she began to craft her own stories from an early age. She aims to encourage, inspire, and educate in her stories.

Based out of Fayetteville North Carolina, Tiffany is originally from Virginia Beach, VA. She is co-founder of Gibbs Publishing Conglomerate.

You can connect with me on:
🌐 https://gibbspublishingconglomerate.com
f https://www.facebook.com/GibbsPublishing

Also by Tiffany Gibbs

Found in the Storm

Found in the Storm by Tiffany and Dameon Gibbs is a gripping fictional narrative that seamlessly weaves together themes of betrayal, forgiveness, redemption, survival, and the testing of one's faith. The authors skillfully crafted an exciting and powerful story that keeps readers on the edge of their seats from start to finish.

The protagonist, Antonio, is a character whose perilous journey forms the backbone of the story. He is a very complex individual with strengths and flaws. His decision to join the Army with the hope of improving his life, only to face a dishonorable discharge, sets the stage for a series of challenges that test his resilience and determination. The story cleverly explores the complexities of Antonio's life as he navigates the aftermath of his choices.

The plot takes a turn when Antonio accepts an under-the-table job flying a helicopter, reminiscent of his military days. The seemingly straightforward task of transporting a package from point A to point B in rural Minnesota becomes a high-stakes adventure, especially when a deadly winter storm sweeps in. The authors create a palpable sense of tension and suspense as Antonio grapples with the decision to risk his life for what initially appeared to be easy money. Will he be able to successfully navigate the helicopter through the blinding, severe snowstorm? How will he survive being on the brink of death?

Tiffany and Dameon Gibbs have created an intriguing tale that is both thrilling and thought provoking, with realistic and multifaceted characters that make them relatable and realistic. This story is not merely a tale of survival; it is a profound exploration of human resilience and the pursuit of redemption.

Found in the Storm is a must-read for those who enjoy traversing the twists and turns of a story with a compelling blend of adventure and suspense. This novel will leave a lasting impact, inviting readers to reflect on the intricate tapestry of life and the choices that shape our destinies.

Him Her & God

In Him, Her and God, husband and wife team, Dameon and Tiffany Gibbs share their perspective on marriage. Drawing from test, trials, and joy experienced, they share how biblical principles have guided their union.

My Life is an Open Book

As a young girl growing up, words became my voice when I couldn't speak or didn't know what to say. Poetry, in many ways, saved my life and kept my sanity. My fourth grade teacher gave me a journal and told me I should write my poetry down because I was good at it. That simple act changed my life.

It is my hope that my struggles and my perseverance will inspire other young women to keep pushing forward. Life as a young girl entering womanhood can be very hard, but you can make it through!

Journey with me from the age of ten into my early adulthood…my family life, school, and even my first relationships.

The Moon is a Piece of Swiss Cheese in the Sky

Tiffany Michele wrote the poem upon which this book is based, ""The Moon's a Piece of Swiss in the Sky"" as a child. Always one with an active imagination, at the request of her husband, she expanded it into a book. Moon's story is one of dealing with loneliness and finding true friendship.